¿Quién me llama?

Learn Peruvian Spanish Slang

by
Daniel McKay

¿Quién me llama? Learn Peruvian Spanish Slang

Version Date 2012.10.16

Print Edition Number 1.1

ISBN : 978-1479218356

Table of Contents

Introduction

To get the absolute best use out of this book having some handle on Spanish will be a real benefit, by this I mean that you can that you can get by, you do not need to be fluent to get the benefit of this book. Although actually, a number of words and phrases will be very useful even if you level of Spanish is low to none existent. If you are planning on learning Spanish in Perú then this book really is the perfect addition.

This book is a collection of Peruanismos, the slang that originates from and which is used day to day on the streets of Perú.

To answer the question why is it important to know the slang in Perú, they speak Spanish after all? Firstly, slang in any Spanish speaking country is such an integral part of the language that is spoken on the streets that in order to make communication that much easier you have to at least know some local slang for whichever country you happen to be in. And, the more you know the better. The more you know and can understand the more fun you will be able to have with locals and the easier it will make things.

Personally, I have a rule of thumb, which is that if I can converse well with an average taxi driver then I am not going to have any problems communicating with anyone in that country. The reason is quite simple (and no offensive to anyone who happens to be a taxi driver by the way) that taxi drivers tend to come from the more common classes and their language tends to be heavily laced with slang.

Despite being fluent in Spanish, I found I was struggling with some of the slang, and I was always asking questions as to the significance of each new slang word. So, I have studied and researched the slang in Perú and written this book to make life easy for anyone else who wants to short cut the learning curve and gain an instant understanding of the slang.

Personally I use a large number of these words day to day in Perú. And, I cannot emphasize enough how much easier it makes communicating with the local people, and in addition all that more enjoyable. Oh, the added benefit is that my Peruvian friends are both shocked and impressed that I can navigate their slang so well. You too can impress in Perú with the help of this book.

Before getting into the slang I want to just explain a little about Spanish in Perú and also how this book is structured.

Firstly, something that you will hear a lot of in Perú is excessive use of the diminutive more often that is most other Spanish speaking countries. It is kind of endearing when you get used to it and it is actually meant very much that way. For example, 'ahora' (now) becomes 'ahorita', animales (animals) become 'animalitos', and so on and on. You will hear this time and time again, even to the point that you end up using this form after not too long.

Secondly, when in a restaurant, a bar or even in the street you will hear people call somebody they don't know 'joven', as in young. Like hey 'joven' can we order some drinks, or hey 'joven' can we get the bill, or whatever. This is used even when speaking to elder people. At first I found it all a little strange, but hey there is no point fighting it, just get used to it.

So how is this book structured? First off, I wanted to keep things as simple as possible, unlike some other slang books with you need to have a matrix to figure out each word. So, all the slang words are in alphabetical order, with a separate chapter for each letter. Next, all the slang words are in capital letters so that they stand out very clearly. For each slang word, there is a translation into English. Following this there is an example of the slang word in Spanish, each time this begins with 'Ex.' for example. After the example in Spanish I have included a translation into English of that example for clarification, which is in brackets. Note, the example in English is how the slang is used, as some of the words will have completely different meanings if a literal translation is taken.

One final note, in some cases both the masculine and feminine forms can be used. In all of these cases the slang word is written in the masculine form and has an (A) to denote that the feminine is also used.

I hope you find this useful and enjoy your time in Perú. It is a country with a rich culture and fantastic food, just be careful with the water.

A

A LA TELA : This is used to say that somebody is very well dressed, elegantly dressed or suited up.

Ex. A esa disoteca tienes que ir a la tela de lo contrario on podrás entrar. (At that disco you have to go very well dressed otherwise you cannot enter.)

ACHICAR : Literally, in the specific case of water this verb means 'to bail out' and in slang it is used to say that you are going to the bathroom. Women often say this in when they are in bars or restaurants in the presence of male company.

Ex. Después de beber mucho pisco sour, necesito ir a achicar. (After drinking a lot of pisco sour, I need to go to the bathroom.)

ACHORADO : This is person with an aggressive, a hostile or a defiant character or conduct. It can best be translated into English as pigheaded.

Ex. No me gusta que tu amigo sea tan achorado. (I don't like that your friend is so pigheaded.)

AGACHADOS : These are economic (cheap) places to eat popular food. 'Agachar' is to crouch down, and the reference is that these types of places do not have any seating, so you either stand or you crouch down.

Ex. No tenía mucha plata pero le metí algo en los agachados. (He did not have much money but he ate something in the 'agachados'.)

AL POLO : To the pole (north or south), this refers to something being very cold. Most commonly this phrase is used to describe drinks.

Ex. Por favor nos traes dos chelas al polo. (Please bring us two very cold beers.)

AL TOQUE : Right now, right away, at this moment, at this instant. This is used to emphasize urgency for an action or a command. For example, in English you would say 'call your mother right away' as in without any hesitation.

Ex. Tienes que venir a la reunión al toque. (You have to come to the meeting right now, without delay).

AMPAYAR : This is to find somebody in undesirable circumstances that they would not want to be seen in. For example being caught doing something that although may no be illegal would certainly be looked down upon. Like not being seen in your best light.

Ex. Los jugadores fueron ampayados tomando chelas antes del partido. (The players were seen drinking beers before the match.)

A PATA : To go somewhere by foot. A 'pata' is actually the foot of an animal, but in slang it is used for people also to describe the action of walking.

Ex. Perdí el micro esta mañana, tuve que ir a pata hasta mi oficina. (I missed the bus this morning, I had to go by foot to the office.)

ARRECHO (A) : To be horny, to be turned on, used with the verb 'estar' (to be).

Ex. Mi novia está arrecha, quiere que vaya a verla al toque. (My girlfriend is horny, she wants that I go and see her right away.)

ARRANCHAR : Replaces 'arrebatar' in Perú, which is to snatch, to seize, usually with force and violently. For example the way a thief would snatch a handbag from a tourist in the street.

Ex. Tengan cuidado con los chorsos, les pueden arranchar la cartera. (Be careful with the thieves, they can snatch your handbag.)

ARRUGA : Literally 'arruga' is a crease or a wrinkle, such as one on the face. However, in slang it is used to describe a debt.

Ex. Tengo una arruga enorme que tengo que cancelar al banco. (I have a huge debt with the bank that I have to clear.)

ASADO : Literally this translates as roast. So it is not a huge stretch of the imagination to see that in slang it refers to somebody who is pissed off, is of bad humor, or quite simply annoyed.

Ex. Mi esposo está asado conmigo porque choqué su carro. (My husband is pissed with me because I crashed his car.)

A SU MADRE : This is a very common expression to show your shock or surprise at something. It actually translates to 'his/her/your mother'. In English it would be replaced by that 'No way!' gasp, that surprised expression of disbelief. Note that it is not actually rude and often it is shortened to just 'a su'.

Ex. El celular me costó 500 dólares. ¡A su madre! (The cell phone cost me 500 dollars. No way!)

AVENTADO : This literally translates as thrown or pushed, however in the slang context it means somebody who is very brave or very daring. The kind of person who willing would do something risky, or scary without a second thought.

Ex. Pablo es tan aventado que sin pensar saltó del cuarto piso, se ha podido matar. (Pablo is so daring that without thinking he jumped from the fourth floor, he could have killed himself.)

B

BACÁN : Cool, great, awesome. This is one of those words you will hear over and over again in Perú. It is used to describe anything out of normal in the positive sense.

Ex. Que bacán los subwoofers de tu nuevo carro. (How awesome the subwoofers are in your new car.)

BAMBA : This is the same as pirated in English, used to describe anything that is an imitation product, most commonly used to describe things such as clothes, DVDs, and books (yes really, books are often photocopied in Perú.). The piracy laws in Perú are not as strong or as heavily enforced as in other countries, and as such, there are many markets where you can buy pirated products.

Ex. Los precios de los productos bamba son más baratos. (The prices of the pirated products are cheaper.)

BICICLETA : Obviously this is a bicycle in English. But, it is used to say that somebody has diarrhea or a bad stomach and has to keep visiting the bathroom.

Ex. No voy a salir estoy con la bicicleta. (I am not going to go out, I have diarrhea.)

BLANCA or BLANQUITA: Literally this mean white (in the case of 'blanca') or little white (in the case of 'blanquita'). It is not too difficult to see why this is used as the slang for cocaine.

Ex. ¿Puedes venderme 30 soles de la blanca? (Can you sell me 30 sols of cocaine?)

BOMBA : Literally this translates as a bomb. In slang 'bomba' means to get really very drunk, it is a shorter version of 'gran borrachera'.

Ex. Hoy tengo resaca porque ayer me metí una bomba. (Today I have a hangover because yesterday I got really drunk.)

BRICHERO (A) : For most single guys arriving in Peru, and particularly in Lima this is one of the first words that they will learn about. 'Brichera', the name actually originates from Cusco, and it specifically refers to gringo hunters, but it includes any foreigner not just gringos. There are several different types of 'brichera', firstly those that just want to be taken out on the town and wined and dined, and then there are those with the more serious ambition of being taken overseas and given a new life.

One thing that you have to be careful with in Perú is assuming that any girl with a foreigner is a 'brichera', this is certainly not the case. It is their predefined goals and the actions taken to achieve them that are what defines a 'brichera'. There are certainly a lot of 'bricheras' in Lima, and many of them will visit the tourist zone in Miraflores hoping to get her ticket out of Perú.

Regarding 'bricheros' these are far more noticeable in places like Cusco where there is quite a lot of competition. They often hang out in the markets with the specific aim of picking up a foreign girl.

Ex. Esa chica es una brichera, la veo con un gringo diferente cada fin de semana. (That girl is a gringo hunter, I see her with a different gringo every weekend.)

BRÓCOLI : Literally this translates the same in English as brocoli, but in Slang it refers to a gay or homosexual guy. As with most slang that refers to sexual preference it is offense.

Ex. En la escuela a tu hermano le dicen brócoli porque mira mucho a los chicos. (In the school they say your brother is gay because he looks a lot at the boys.)

BRÓDER : This is taken directly from the English word brother and is used as such in the colloquial sense of 'amigo' or friend.

Ex. Después de estudiar tantos años juntos el se convirtió en mi mejor bróder. (After studying so many years together he became my best friend.)

C

CABRO or CABRILLA: This refers to an effeminate man, and can also be interchanged with gay or homosexual. Once again this is used as an insult.

Ex. Estoy seguro que el esposo de Juana es cabro, lo vi besándose con un tipo. (I am sure that Juana's husband is gay, I saw him kissing a guy.)

CACHACIENTO : This is to make fun of, joke around, or to simply be sarcastic. It can be interchanged with 'burlón', which comes from 'burlar' (to make fun of or to evade).

Ex. No seas cachaciento y ayuda a recoger los platos que se cayeron. (Don't be joking around and help pick up the plates that fell.)

CACHAR : Literally this translates as 'to catch', it is very similar to 'coger' and has the same meaning in slang that 'coger' has in Argentina for example, which is to have sex.

Ex. ¿Ayer te fuiste a cachar con la chica que conociste en el bar? (Yesterday did you shag the girl that you met in the bar?)

CACHARRO : This means face, it is exactly the same as 'cara' or 'rostro' and can used in the same contexts, although more often it is used in a joking fashion.

Ex. Tú y tu hermana tienen el mismo cacharro. (You and your sister have the same face.)

CACHUELO : This is temporary or informal work. Often the kind of thing that people are paid cash in hand for, no questions asked.

Ex. Pablo está buscando un cachuelo solo por dos semanas. (Pablo is looking for a temporary job for only two weeks.)

CAIDO DEL PALTO : Literally translated as 'fallen from the avocado tree' this infers somebody has had a knock on the head and means that they are disturbed, cannot pay attention or simply they are just a bit stupid.

Ex. Carlos es muy distraído siempre anda caido del palto. (Carlos is very disturbed, he is always confused.)

CALABAZA : The literal translation is Pumpkin. Because a pumpkin is pretty much empty inside this word is used to describe 'airheads', 'blondes' (in the sense of dumb) or any other girl considered to be dim.

Ex. Las chicas no entienden lo que el profesor está explicando, son muy calabazas. (Those girls don't understand what the teacher is explaining, they are airheads.)

CALATO (A) : This means nude or naked, it is actually commonly used.

Ex. No estoy lista para salir, porque aún estoy calata. (I am not ready to go out, because I am still naked.)

CALDERO : Literally a caldron, this is the term used to describe the after effects of getting drunk, that feeling ill the follow day. The caldron refers to the stomach, hence it's relevance.

Ex. Vamos a comer algo para apagar el caldero, anoche hemos chupado demasiado. (Let's go eat something to quench the caldron, last night we drank too much.)

CAMOTUDO (A) : This is somebody that falls in love very easily, it is used in place of 'enamoradizo'.

Ex. Jose es muy camotudo, apenas la conoce y ya quiere casarse. (Jose falls in love far to easily, he hardly knows her and already he wants to marry her.)

CANCEROSO : Cancerous, this can almost only mean one thing, yeap, it is another name for a cigarette.

Ex. La entravista fue bien sólo falta un canceroso para los nervios. (The interview went well, only needed a cigarette for the nerves.)

CANCHITA : In Perú this is the word for popcorn. It seems most Spanish speaking countries have their own specific name for popcorn.

Ex. Es rico comer canchita mientras veo una pelicula. (It is yummy to eat popcorn while I watch a movie.)

CANA : This means prison in slang. Instead of saying 'carcel' you can just say that somebody is in the 'cana'. Note the literal translation for 'cana' is a white hair, as in a hair on somebodies head. I guess if you are in prison long enough you will end up with white hairs.

Ex. Los choros que sean atrapados por la policía serán llevados a cana. (The thieves caught by the police will be taken to prison.)

CAÑA : Despite actually meaning cane as a literal translation in Spanish 'caña' is the slang word used to call a car.

Ex. Paola tiene una nueva caña. (Paola has a new car.)

CARRETÓN : This is to describe a strong sexual appetite or desire.

Ex. Después de 30 días sin ver mujeres vengo recontra carretón. (After 30 days without seeing women I have a huge sexual desire.)

CAUSA : Although this is also the name of a local dish in Perú it also is used to describe a close friend, but only male to male friends say this. This is also mainly used only in the lower classes.

Ex. Miguel es mi causa, lo conozco desde que tenía doce años. (Miguel is my friend, I have known him since I was twelve years old.)

COCA COLA : This one almost rhymes perfectly actually. It is used to refer to somebody as crazy ('loco' for a guy or 'loca' for a girl).

Ex. Tu hermana es coca cola, siempre hace cosas extrañas. (Your sister is crazy, she is always doing strange things.)

COIMA : This is actually used in a number of Spanish speaking countries, Perú included. It means a bribe.

Ex. Tuve que dar una coima a la policia para evitar la multa. (I had to give a bride to the police to avoid the fine.)

COMBI : These are the large vans that are used as buses around the cities. In Lima for example you will see hundreds of these combi's, with the fare collectors touting for business. Generally they can hold around 25 to 40 passengers.

Ex. Tengo que tomar dos combis para llegar a mi trabajo. (I have to take two buses to get to my job.)

COMO CANCHA : Like a football pitch, well as you can imagine this is used to describe a huge quantity or volume. It can be used equally to describe a large number of people, or a lot of food for example.

Ex. Había como cancha de gente en el concierto. (There were a lot of people at the concert.)

COCHO (A) : This is one of the many ways of saying old in Perú. It is used to refer to people as opposed to objects.

Ex. Mi abuelo es muy cocho para hacer ese tipo de trabajo. (My grandfather is very old to do that type of work.)

COJUDO (A) : This is a fairly strong insult which roughly translates as idiot or dumb ass.

Ex. ¡Que cojuda fue esa mujer al perdonarle esa infidelidad! (What a dumb ass that women was for forgiving him for his infidelity!)

CONCHUDO : This is shameless, or a rascal, or somebody who simply does nor care about the opinion of others. This can be used to call the kind of person who leaves a bar or restaurant without paying the bill.

Ex. Jorge es tan conchudo que no le importa lo que le digan. (Jorge es so shameless that he does not care what they say to him.)

COSTILLA : Literally meaning, rib it is used in place of 'novia' (girlfriend). It comes from Eve being created from the rib of Adam.

Ex. Mi costilla siempre me molesta porque la casa esta sucia. (My girlfriend is always bothering me because the house is dirty.)

CUERO : As a literal translation this means leather. It is used to replace 'guapo', or 'lindo', as in a very handsome man.

Ex. El protagonista de la película es muy cuero. (The protagonist of the movie is very handsome.)

CH

CHAIRA : A 'navaja' or a 'cuchilla', or in English a knife, or penknife, or pocket knife.

Ex. Tenga cuidado porque los choros llevan chairas. (Be careful because the thieves carry knives.)

CHAMBA : This is just like saying 'trabajo' which means work.

Ex. No encuentro chamba en ningun lado.(I don't find work anywhere.)

CHANCHA : This is a collection between friends so that something can be paid for collectively, like a party or a barbecue for example.

Ex. Hagamos una chancha para comprar tragos para celebrar el fin de los exámenes. (Lets make a collection to buy drinks to celebrate the end of the exams.)

CHANCLETERO : This is a guy that only has daughters, he has no sons. Latin culture is very macho, hence the fact there is slang for this.

Ex. Mi tío es un chancletero porque tiene cuarto hijas. (My uncle is a 'chancletero' becuase he has four daughters.)

CHANCÓN : This is somebody who is very studious and hardworking. A good translation to English would be nerd.

Ex. Jorge es chancón, siempre está estudiendo y tiene altas notas en todos sus exámenes. (Jorge is a nerd, he is always studying and has good grades in all of his exams.)

CHARAPA : This is a type of turtle found in the Amazonia region of Perú. This is not an offensive or derogatory term used to describe anyone from the jungle in Perú.

Ex. Mi amiga charapa vendrá a la ciudad esta fin de semana. (My jungle friend will come to the city this weekend.)

CHATO (A) : Used to describe somebody as short. Often used in a playful manner between friends, sometimes used even as a nickname.

Ex. Nos parece chatas por al costado de Carla, ella es alta. (We look short beside Carla, she is tall.)

CHATURRI : This has the same meaning as 'chato' which is a short person. Not used quite as much as 'chato' though.

Ex. Natalia es chaturri, ella es más chata que todos sus compañeros. (Natalia is very short, she is shorter than all of her colleagues.)

CHAUFA : This is used in place of ciao or see you later in Perú. This is a quick way of saying goodbye.

Ex. Laura, ya tengo que irme, chaufa. (Laura, I have to go no, ciao, see you later.)

CHELA : A beer, it is not a brand of beer, rather just a name for beer. You may find yourself getting invited for a couple of beers (un par de chelas) if you are lucky.

Ex. Vamos a tomar un par de chelas. (Lets go have a couple of beers.)

CHÉVERE : A word to describe something as cool, great or awesome. 'Chévere' is interchangeable with 'bacán'.

Ex. Qué chévere que vengas a la fiesta esta noche. (How great that you come to the party tonight.)

CHIBOLO : This is another word you will hear a very often in Perú. It means a young person, basically somebody in their teens. It is not at all offensive.

Ex. Mira hay cinco chibolos bailando en la calle. (Look there are five teenagers dancing in the street.)

CHIBOLERO (A) : A man or women who dates someone a lot younger than themselves.

Ex. Mi tía es una chibolera, siempre sale con tipos mas de viente años menor de su edad. (My aunt is a 'chibolera', she always goes out with guys more than twenty years younger than her.)

CHIFA : This has two closely related meanings in Perú, firstly it means Chinese food, and secondly, it means Chinese restaurant. In fact if you first arrive in Lima airport and head into the city you cannot fail but notice the large number of restaurants that have CHIFA on their signs. All of these are as you guessed it, Chinese restaurants.

Ex. La chifa en Perú es muy rica. (The Chinese food in Perú is very good.)

CHILINDRINAS : Another word for beers (cervezas). Not quite as commonly used, as 'chela' but is equally interchangeable.

Ex. Porfa nos traiga tres chilindrinas. (Please bring us three beers.)

CHINA : This is the 50 centimos coin. Centimos are the equivalent of cents to a dollar, there are 100 centimos in one Sol.

Ex. No puedo crearlo, hay que pagar una china para usar el baño en el supermercado. (I cannot believe it, one has to pay 50 centimos in order to use the toilets in the super market.)

CHIMBOMBO : This yet another name for a homosexual. Once again, it is somewhat offensive depending on the context.

Ex. Con esa ropa parece chimbombo. (With those clothes you look gay.)

CHOBORRA : This is a play on the letter order. By moving 'cho' from the end of the word 'borracho' to the front, we have a different word in slang, which also happens to mean drunk.

Ex. Mi tío fue choborra anoche, no se dio cuenta que estaba haciendo. (My uncle was drunk last night, he did not realize what he was doing.)

CHOCHE : Another word which is used for friend in Perú. This can be a male or female friend.

Ex. Mi choche va a llamarme esta noche. (My friend is going to call me tonight.)

CHOCOLLO : This is somebody that lacks guts or the balls to do something. Like a wimp or a wuss.

Ex. Eres un chocollo, deberías decirle a Paola que te ama. (You are wuss, you should tell Paola that you love her.)

CHOMPA : In Perú this is the name used for a sweater or a jumper.

Ex. Deberías llevar tu chompa hoy porque hace frío. (You should wear your sweater today because it is cold.)

CHONGO : This has a couple of uses in Perú. Firstly if can be used to say whorehouse, and secondly it can be used to describe confusion or chaos.

Ex. Juan no va al chongo, porque tiene una novia. (Juan does not go to the whorehouse, because he has a girlfriend.)

CHOQUE Y FUGA : This is a one night stand. Literally meaning to crash and then escape.

Ex. No sé el nombre completo del padre de mi hija, fue un choque y fuga. (I don't know the complete name of the father of my daughter, it was a one night stand.)

CHORO : In other Spanish speaking countries you will be used to hearing the word 'ladron' for thief, but in Perú they call thieves 'choros'.

Ex. El choro se escapó antes de que la policía pudo arrestarlo. (The thief escaped before the police could arrest him.)

CHUCHA : This is one of the slang words which is used to describe the female sexual organ, the vagina. This is a pretty coarse word as you can imagine.

Ex. La chucha de Elena tiene un huele muy horrible. (Elena's vagina smells really bad.)

CHUNGO : This is a tightwad. There are other words that can also be used, such as 'duro' or 'tacaño'.

Ex. Mi hermano nunca deja una propina en un restaurante, es chungo. (My brother never leaves a tip in restaurant, he is a tightwad.)

CHUPA MEDIAS : This translates as somebody who sucks socks, which in turn means a kiss ass. This is not limited to Perú by any means but it is used.

Ex. Paola es una chupa medias, siempre está regalando cosas al profesor. (Paola is a kiss ass, she is always giving gifts to the teacher.)

CHUPAR : Literally in Spanish this means to suck. However, it is used in the context of drinking alcohol in Perú. In place of 'tomar' you will hear 'chupar' especially amongst groups of friends.

Ex. Vamos a chupar esta viernes para celebrar el cumpleaños de Mario. (We are going to drink this Friday to celebrate Mario's birthday.)

CHUPÓDROMO : This is a bar, or anywhere that people come together solely for the purpose of drinking alcohol.

Ex. Anoche fuimos a chupar en el chupódromo cerca de tu casa. (Last night we went to drink in the bar near your house.)

CHURRO : This is an attractive or handsome man. It can be roughly translated to hunk in English. However, churro is actually a fried strip of dough, sold almost everywhere in Perú and the rest of Latin America.

Ex. El hermano de Laura es un churro. (Laura's brother is a hunk.)

CHUSO (A) : Meaning how ordinary, how common, how disgusting or how revolting. This replaces '¡que asco!' in Perú.

Ex. ¿Por qué dices esas palabras? ¡Qué chuso eres! (Why do you say those words? How disgusting you are!)

CRUDO : The literal translation is underdone or raw, which is just how a white person looks in Perú. Most often this is used to refer to a gringo.

Ex. Casi todos los gringos que vienen a Perú por sus vacaciones son crudos. (Almost all the gringos that come to Perú for their holiday are white.)

D

DAR EN EL CLAVO : This is a little more than to guess correctly (acertar), it best translates as to hit the nail on the head.

Ex. Pablo dio en el clavo que Elena no pudo recordar su nombre. (Pablo hit the nail on the head that Elena could not remember his name.)

DAR SAJIRO : This is to give the possibility or to give an advantage to somebody. For example you give someone a 5 seconds head start on you in a race.

Ex. Empieza si quieres te voy a dar sajiro 5 segundos. (Start if you want, I am going to give you 5 seconds head start.)

DE BOLETO : This is same as 'trasnochar' which means to stay up all night from one day until the next without sleep.

Ex. Juan la siguió de largo y se fue a la escuela de boleto. (Juan stayed up all night and went to school without any sleep.)

DE FRESA : Used in place of 'de frente', meaning straight ahead.

Ex. La tienda que buscas esta de fresa. (The shop you are looking for is straight ahead.)

DE TODAS MANGAS : This is used to say something that is inevitable, or no matter what in any case it will happen.

Ex. De todas mangas estaremos allí, no podemos faltar una reunion tan importante. (In any case we will be there, we cannot miss such an important meeting.)

DOBLE FILO : The literal translation is 'double edged', and as such it is not too hard to understand that is a way of calling somebody bisexual.

Ex. Tu hermano es doble filo, tiene una novia y un novio. (Your brother is bisexual, he has a girlfriend and a boyfriend.)

DURO : Literally meaning hard or tough, this is also a word used to call somebody a tightwad ('tacaño' or 'chungo').

Ex. Mi padre es duro, no me prestó nada para comprar un carro. (My father is a tightwad, he didn't loan me anything to buy a car.)

E

EN BOLA : This is a way of saying that a women is pregnant, 'embarazada' in Spanish.

Ex. Carla está en bola, por eso no viene a trabajar. (Carla is pregnant, because of this she does not come to work.)

ENTRE PISCO Y NAZCA : This is quite a nice way of saying that somebody is drunk.

Ex. No creo que Jose pueda llegar a su casa, está entre pisco y nazca. (I don't think that Jose can make it to his house, he is drunk.)

ENYUCAR : This is to cheat, swindle or con somebody. It is used in place of 'timar' or 'engañar'.

Ex. Juan compró un carro a plazos y está enyucado por 3 años. (Juan bought a car on credit and he is getting ripped off for 3 years.)

ESTIRAR LA PATA : To stretch the leg which is a nice way of saying (morir) to die.

Ex. Tristement anoche mi abuelo estiró la pata. (Sadly last night my grandfather died.)

F

FALLO : This is used to call a cigarette or tobacco.

Ex. ¿Me prestas un fallo porfa? (Can you loan me a cigarette?)

FEDERICO (A) : Can be used in both the masculine and feminine forms to call somebody ugly.

Ex. Elena es federica, es increíble que tiene un novio, él debería ser ciego. (Elena is really ugly, it is increible that she has a boyfriend, he must be blind.)

FERCHO : This is a play on the letters in the word, for 'chofer', by moving them around you get 'fercho'. Both mean exactly the same which in English is driver or chauffeur.

Ex. El fercho va a recogernos a las siete. (The driver is going to collect us at seven o'clock.)

FIGURETI : This means somebody who is a show off or a poser, or even a wannabe.

Ex. Monica es figureti, siempre está de fresa la camera. (Monica is a poser, she is always in front of the camera.)

FLACO (A) : Literally meaning that somebody is thin or skinny this is yet another way to say boyfriend or girlfriend.

Ex. Debo irme ahorita, voy a encontrar mi flaco al cine. (I must go now, I am going to meet my boyfriend at the cinema.)

FLOREAR : To praise, flatter, or even lie in a complimentary manner.

Ex. Raul le estaba floreando a Paola porque le gusta mucho. (Raul was flattering Paola because he likes her a lot.)

FLORO : Taken from the slang verb 'florear' this means a lie.

Ex. Francisco nos dijo un floro, no es verdad que perdió su reloj, lo vendió. (Francisco told us a lie, it is not true that he lost his watch, he sold it.)

FRITO : Literally meaning fried this is not exactly politically correct but it is used in Perú to call a black person.

Ex. En Perú hay más fritos que viven en la selva que en Lima. (In Peru there are more blacks that live in the jungle than in Lima.)

FUMÓN : This word is derived from the verb 'fumar' which is to smoke and in this case it refers to a pot head, somebody that smokes marihuana.

Ex. Raul es un fumón, siempre fuma marijuana. (Raul is a pot head, he is always smoking marihuana.)

G

GIL : This is somebody who is mentally slow, or stupid. Dimwit makes a good translation into English.

Ex. Pablo es tan gil que no se dá cuenta que su novia lo engaña. (Pablo is such a dimwit that he does not realize that his girlfriend is cheating him.)

GRIFO : No, unlike in Spain this does not mean tap. Well, it sort of does I guess. In Perú 'Grifo' means gas or petrol station. Everybody I have ever heard in Perú calls gas stations 'grifos', which is a bit shorter then the official name 'gasolinera'.

Ex. El cana no tiene mucho gas, voy al grifo para llenarlo. (The car doesn't have much gas, I am going to the gas station in order to fill it up.)

GRINGO : A fairly obvious one, but just as a clarification that this only refers to North Americans in Perú, unlike in some other countries where the term gringo refers to any westerner. It is not an offensive term in Perú.

Ex. Los gringos gastan mas plata que la gente de acá. (The North Americans spend more money than the people from here.)

GRONE : Once again this is a play on the letters in a word, this time for 'negro' meaning a black person. It is a little offensive.

Ex. ¿Por qué te gusta, es grone? (Why do you like him, he is black?)

H

HABLAR POR LOS CODOS : To talk for the elbows is how this literally translates and it is an expression to say that somebody is talking way too much.

Ex. Mi esposa me hablaba por los codos, me volvió loco. (My wife was talking way to much, she drove me crazy.)

HACER LA PUFI : This is way of saying to have a crap or have a shit.

Ex. Después de comer tanta comida quiero hacer la pufi. (After eating so much food I want to take a shit.)

HACER LA TABA : This best translates as to accompany somebody. Can be used in place of the verb to accompany 'acompañar'.

Ex. Te haré la taba hasta la casa de tu primo. (I will accompany you until your cousin's house.

HACER GOL : To make a goal. Well, this refers to getting a girl or women pregnant.

Ex. Estoy feliz porque hice gol a mi esposa. (I am happy because I got my wife pregnant.)

HACER PILA : To do a battery, since batteries leak, you got it, this means to take a piss, go for a wee, to urinate, to take a leak.

Ex. No debe hacer pila en la piscina. (You must not urinate in the swimming pool.)

HACERSE BOLAS : This is to see a problem where there is actually no problem at all.

Ex. No te hagas bolas, el choque no ha sido fuerte. (Don't see problems that are not there, the crash was not hard.)

HEMBRITA : Yet another word referring to a female partner, wife or girlfriend. This is used in a sentimental sense, as it ends in 'ita', kind of like saying honey in English.

Ex. Mi hembrita le gusta ir al cine. (My honey likes to go to the cinema.)

HUACHAFO (A) : This is a person that has very bad or very poor taste. For example, somebody that wears ridiculous clothing that do not match.

Ex. Alejandra es tan huachafa que nadie quiere salir con ella. (Alejandra has such bad taste that nobody wants to go out with her.)

HUACHIMÁN : A kind of cross from the English for Watchman, and it means exactly that, 'watchman'. These are private guards, often installed in apartment buildings, shops or even in the streets at night in say gated communities. The other words in Spanish used to describe 'huachiman' are 'vigilante' or 'guardián'.

Ex. El huachimán me dijo que había un serpiente en el jardin. (The watchman told me that there was a snake in the garden.)

HUASCA : Another way of describing being drunk.

Ex. ¿Si estás huasca cómo vas a manejar tu carro? (If you are drunk how are you going to drive your car?)

HUECO (A) : Literally this translates as a hole. As you can imagine this is used to refer to somebody as empty headed, an air-head, or a stereotypical blonde for example.

Ex. Patricia es una hueca, no sabe como usar su celular. (Patricia is an air-head, she does not know how to use her cell phone.)

HUEVÓN : This is another very common expression, actually it is used in a number of Spanish speaking countries to call somebody and idiot, a dumb ass or a fool.

Ex. El forcho es un huevón, maneja muy mal y peligrosamente. (The driver is an idiot, he drives very badly and dangerously.)

HUIRO : This is a joint, a cigarette of marijuana.

Ex. Con un huiro se puede relajarse. (With a joint one can relax.)

J

JALAR : Literally this translates as to pull, it is normally used in place of 'tirar' in South America ('tirar' being used in Spain). However, in slang it is to flunk, or fail. An example is to fail your exams.

Ex. Mi padre está enojado conmigo porque he jalado mis exámenes. (My father is angry with me because I have failed my exams.)

JALE : This also comes from the verb 'jalar' and is the command to pull, which you will see on the doors of most shops in South America. It is used in slang to define a person's pulling power, attractiveness or sex appeal.

Ex. Pablo tiene jale, nunca tiene problemas conocer chicas. (Pablo has pulling power, he never has problems meeting girls.)

JAMA : This is a word for food. It is just like saying 'comida' in Perú.

Ex. Quiero jama porque tengo hambre. (I want food because I am hungry.)

JAMEAR : Used as a verb to eat (comer).

Ex. Tengo mucho hambre, vamos a jamear. (I am very hungry, lets go eat.)

JATEAR : This is a slang verb which means to sleep, to rest or at least to siesta. Note that there is also another way of saying this in slang and that is 'tirar jato' which is to pull home.

Ex. Estoy cansado, voy a jatear un rato en mi jato. (I am tired, I am going to sleep for short while in my house.)

JATO : Another very commonly used word in Perú, this means house or home.

Ex. Voy a llamar Pedro por teléfone cuando llegue a mi jato. (I am going to call Pedro by phone when I arrive at my house.)

JERMA : Yes, yet another term used to describe a girlfriend, female lover or even wife.

Ex. Mi jerma es muy celosa, no me deja hablar a otras chicas en la calle. (My girl is very jealous, she doesn't let me speak to other girls in the street.)

JONCA : This is specifically a box of beer (una caja de cerveza), not a six pack but a box, normally these have 24 bottles or cans.

Ex. Voy a traer dos joncas a la fiesta esta noche. (I am going to bring two crates of beer to the party tonight.)

JUERGA : This is a binge, a rave up, a party. It can be used interchangeable with 'tono' or 'fiesta'.

Ex. Va a estar una buena juerga esta noche, hay much gente que va a venir. (It is going to be a good party today, there are a lot of people who are going to come.)

JUERGEAR : This is to party, to have a rave up, to binge. It is interchangeable with 'tonear'.

Ex. Tuve un día malísimo, vamos a juergear, así podrá olvidar todo lo que pasó hoy. (I had an awful day, lets go and party, like this I will be able to forget everything that happened today.)

JUGADOR (A) : This translates as player, both in the male and female sense. It is not too hard to understand that in slang it means a womanizer for a man and a promiscuous woman, for well, a woman.

Ex. Juan es un jugador, tiene tres novias al mismo tiempo. (Juan is a womanizer, he has three girlfriends at the same time.)

K

KEKE : This is the ass, not the sense of a donkey but the 'culo', a person's ass.

Ex. Juana tiene un gran keke, pero en todo caso me gusta su keke. (Juana has a big ass, but in any case I like her ass.)

L

LA HIZO LINDA : This expression is used when something was achieved under the best possible conditions.

Ex. Paola se fue a Canadá, se casó con un guapo, millonario y que la quiere mucho, la hizo linda. (Paola went to Canada, she married a very handsome millionaire and he loves her a lot, she hit the jackpot.)

LADRILLO : Literally it translates as brick, as in the type of brick used to construct a house. As it is workers that build houses using bricks, 'ladrillo' has come to replace 'trabajador' or 'obrero' in Perú.

Ex. Hoy, los ladrillos llegaron tarde a la obra. (Today, the workers arrived late to the job.)

LATEAR : This is a made up slang verb meaning to walk. It is interchangeable with 'caminar', which is to walk in Spanish.

Ex. Voy a latear hasta la escuela. (I am going to walk to the school.)

LECHERO : Somebody who is very lucky or fortunate is a 'lechero'. It literally translates as milkman.

Ex. Juan es lechero, solo había un premio y se lo ganó. (Juan is lucky, there was only one prize and he won it.)

LENTEJA : Translates literally as 'lentil'. In slang this refers to somebody as mentally slow or stupid, not quite a 'tonto' or fool but on similar lines.

Ex. Pablo es una lenteja, siempre tengo que explicar tres veces antes de que le entender. (Pablo is slow, I always have to explain three times to him before he understands.)

LOMPA : These are trousers. Or 'pantalones' in Spanish.

Ex. Un buen lompa para esta chompa, y quedo listo para juergear. (A good pair of trousers for the this jumper, and I am ready to party.)

LORNA : Another form of calling somebody a fool, a dummy, silly or stupid.

Ex. Que lorna eres, cómo te has dejado robar tu carro. (What a fool you are, how have you allowed your car to be stolen.)

LUCA : This is the equivalent of 1 SOL, the national currency of Perú.

Ex. Tengo 50 lucas para todo al fin de semana. (I have 50 soles for the whole weekend.)

M

MACHONA : This means lesbian. It is derived from Macho, hence infers that the girl or woman is macho in characteristics.

Ex. Mi tía es una machona, pero, por lo menos su novia es una mamacita. (My aunt is a lesbian, but, at least her girlfriend is hot.)

MAMACITA : Just like saying 'guapa' or 'linda', this is a very positive, a very complimentary word to use for a girl or women meaning that she is very beautiful, or very hot. And this is a word the girls love to hear.

Ex. Tu amiga Gabriela es una mamacita, me tienes que presentarle. (Your friend Gabriela is a very beautiful, you have to introduce me to her.)

MANCAR : Another way to say 'morir', to die, or it can also be used in the context of to fall into disgrace also.

Ex. Juan mancó, perdió todo su plata en la bolsa de valores. (Juan became disgraced, he lost all his money in the stock market.)

MAÑOSO (A) : This is a person who is perverted, or and has improper sexual conduct.

Ex. El mañoso de mi primo le gusta mirar los pechos de mi amiga. (My perverted cousin likes to look at the breasts of my friend.)

MANYA : This is used in place of 'mira' or 'observa', used to draw attention to something or someone. In English, we would say 'hey look'. You will hear this a lot especially between groups of friends to highlight something special or unusual.

Ex. Manya a ese hombre, que cuero es. (Look at that man, how handsome he is.)

MARIACHI : In Perú this is used not to refer to a musician but to the partner of a women, as in her boyfriend or a husband.

Ex. Paola no es soltera, tiene su mariachi. (Paola is not single, she has her man.)

MARICÓN : This is a fairly common insult, used to call somebody gay, queer or homosexual.

Ex. ¡Eres un maricón! Te he visto besando un tipo. (You are gay! I saw you kissing a guy.)

MARIQUITA : This, just like 'maricón' is a fairly common insult, used to call somebody gay, queer or homosexual. However, it is also sometimes used playfully between friends instead of saying 'hey buddy' you may hear 'hey gay'.

Ex. ¿Oye mariquita, que hiciste la semana pasada? (Hey queer, what did you do last week?)

MICA : This is used to abbreviate 'camisa', or shirt in English.

Ex. Me gusta tu mica, es bacán. (I like your shirt, it's cool.)

MICRO : This is a small passenger bus, the same thing as a 'combi'.

Ex. Es necesario tomar el micro hasta el centro de la cuidad porque no hay taxis acá en esta cuidad. (It is nessecary to take the bus to the centre of the city because there are no taxis in this city.)

MISIO : Broke, as in not having any money, or you can even use it to say somebody is poor.

Ex. Estoy misio, no tengo ninguna luca. (I am broke, I don't have a single sol.)

MITRA : Somebody's head , or in Spanish 'cabaza'.

Ex. Susana tiene un dolor de mitra que se le hace insoportable. (Susana has a headache that she finds unbearable.)

MONSE : This is the equivalent of 'tonto' or 'ingenuo'. Basically, this means stupid, as in a stupid person.

Ex. Eres monse, porque compraste esta cadena, no es de plata, te han estafado. (You are stupid, why did you buy that chain, it is not silver, they cheated you.)

N

NANCY : A way of saying nothing, or 'nada' in Spanish.

Ex. No sé nancy. (I know nothing.)

Ñ

ÑATA : Translates as nose or 'nariz' in Spanish.

Ex. Con esta ñata me parece como un loro. (With that nose he looks like a parrot.)

ÑOBA : Once again, the letters are switched around to mean the same thing. In this case the letters of 'baño' (bathroom).

Ex. La ñoba queda atrás del restaurante. (The bathroom is behind the restaurant.)

ÑORSA : This means wife 'mujer' or 'esposa in Spanish.

Ex. La ñorsa de Pablo es dentista. (Pablo's wife is a dentist.)

P

PAJA : If you know slang from other Spanish speaking countries you will instantly recognize this as meaning something else (wank or masturbate). However, as you find in many Spanish speaking countries a slang word in one country can have a completely different meaning in an other country, and this is exactly the case here. 'Paja' refers to something as cool, good or excellent.

Ex. Voy a comprarme una mica paja que acabo de ver en el mercado. (I am going to buy myself a cool shirt that I just saw in the market.)

PAJEAR : Now this is the verb use to masturbate in Perú. The word for a wanker is 'pajero', and this like in English is an insult. But it is also used joking between friends.

Ex. No tenía suerte con las chicas esta noche, me voy a pajear ahora. (I had no luck with the girls tonight, I am going to masturbate now.)

PALERO : This is used to describe a person who is a liar, or a loud mouth or just somebody that makes up stories.

Ex. No escuche a las cuentas de Raul, es palero, no se puede crear ninguna de sus cuentas. (Don't listen to Raul's stories, he is a liar, one cannot believe any of his stories.)

PALTA : The literal translation is avocado in slang. 'Palta' is used to describe shame, embarrassment, not as commonly used as 'roche' but it also translates best to 'vergüenza' in Spanish.

Ex. Me caí en la calle, que palta. (I fell over in the street, how embarrassing.)

PAPAYA : Used to refer to the female sexual organ, or lets just be blunt about this, it is the same as saying pussy in English.

Ex. Los soperos les gustan las papayas. (The pussy eaters like the pussy's.)

PATA : This is a common word used to describe a friend in Perú. Except that is this case it means that it is a very good friend.

Ex. Juan es mi pata desde la escuela hace unos años. (Juan is my friend since school from some years ago.)

PAVO : This actually translates as turkey and it can be used to describe somebody as clumsy or foolish.

Ex. Pedro es tan pavo que en la fiesta se escondió. (Pedro is such a turkey that he hid at the party.)

PENDEJO (A) : Yet another insult, not as strong as in some other Spanish speaking countries (Mexico being one). 'Pendejo' refers to a sharp sly untrustworthy person.

Ex. Raul es un pendejo, no le presta plata. (Raul is sly and untrustworthy, don't loan him money.)

PESCADO : Literally this is a fish. Like with any fish the best bit is the body, and you throw the head away. As such this is how to describe a girl who has a great body but ugly face, if you ignore the face (head) it is really good.

Ex. Ella es un pescado, su cuerpo es increíble pero su cara es fea. (She is a fish, her body is amazing but her face is ugly.)

PICHANGA : This is an informal game of football, a pick up game of football between friends for example.

Ex. Lo siento mamá, estoy tarde porque hicimos una pichanga en el parque. (Sorry mom, I am late because we had a kick around in the park.)

PIÑA : With a literal Spanish translation of pineapple this can surely only mean bad luck or misfortune.

Ex. Soy una piña, no he ganado ningún premio en toda mi vida. (I am so unlucky, I have not won any prize in all my life.)

PIRAÑAS : Literally this translates as piranhas which equates to a bunch of young kids who are thieves. In the centre of Lima you will see these kind of kids running around the markets, just something to be aware of.

Ex. Tenga cuidado en el centro de Lima, hay pirañas en los mercados. (Be careful in the centre of Lima, there are young thieves in the markets.)

PISADO : This is an interesting one, for me anyway. Clearly this is the past tense of 'pisar', which is to step on in Spanish. However, in slang this refers to a completely whipped man. I mean whipped in the sense that he does every single thing his wife or girlfriend tells him to do. Not just like taking out the trash, but far beyond that.

Ex. Mi esposo es pisado, le dije a limpiar el suelo con un pañuelo y lo hizo. (My husband is whipped, I told him to clean the floor with a tissue and he did it.)

PITO : This is somebody that have never had sexual relations, i.e. is a virgin.

Ex. Juana es tan fea que va a morir pito. (Juana is so ugly that she is going to die a virgin.)

PITUCO : This is a wealthy or rich person, it also infers that they are snobbish and stuck up. It is a term, which is used as an insult.

Ex. Pablo es pituco, nunca nos saluda en la calle cuando está con sus amigos. (Pablo is stuck up, he never greets us in the street when he is with his friends.)

POLLADA : This is a neighbourhood party, chicken is the main dish. Normally this is a BBQ and used to collect money for family members who are in need.

Ex. Mi primo necesita ayuda para pagar su matricula de la universidad. Vamos a tener una pollada con toda la familia para ayudarle. (My cousin needs helps to pay his university fees. We are going to have a BBQ to help him.)

PONCHO : A rain jacket, well in this case this slang is a rain jacket for the penis, as in a condom.

Ex. Para evitar estar en bola hay que usar un poncho. (To avoid being pregnant one must use a condom.)

PONJA : Another play on the letter order in the word for 'Japon' (Japan in English) which clearly means Japonese.

Ex. Es facil encuentra la buena jama ponja en Lima porque el pescado es rico. (It is easy to find good Japanese food in Lima because the fish is very good.)

POR LAS PURAS : This is to do something for no good reason, or to describe doing something that was a waste of time. For example, spending an hour on a bus to get to the museum to find out that it was closed when you got there.

Ex. Fuimos al centro de Lima por las puras, el museo fue cerrado ese día. (We went to the centre of Lima for nothing, the museum was closed that day.)

PORFA : As in other spanish speaking countries Por Favor (meaning 'please') is often shortened to porfa, it is less of a mouth full to say.

Ex. Dame un cafe con crema, porfa. (Give me a coffee with cream please.)

PROFE : Another contraction of a word, this time for Profesor or Profesora (teacher). Not normally used in a negative sense, more often used in an friendly reminiscent kind of way.

Ex. Mi profe me enseñó mucho sobre la guerra mondial (My teacher taught me a lot about the world war.)

PUCHA : Used as a replacement for the English of 'jeez', or 'grrr' or 'uff'. It is an expression of mild annoyance or irritation. Can also be used to replace 'puta' in expressions to hide that fact you are saying puta. This is more often used by kids, so their parents don't punish them for swearing (saying 'puta').

Ex. ¡Pucha! ¿Y ahora qué voy a hacer? (Jeez! And now what am I going to do?)

R

RAJAR : The correct use of this verb in Spanish is to crack, to rip or to tear. In slang it is used to describe the action of speaking bad about somebody when they are not present. In English we say speaking about somebody behind their back.

Ex. Esa mujer sólo sirve para rajar de su mejor amiga. (That women only talks trash about her best friend.)

RAJÓN (A) : The person that speaks badly about somebody behind their back. Note the reference to 'rajar'.

Ex. Ana es una rajóna, habla mal de sus amigos. (Ana is a 'rajóna' she speaks badly about her friends.)

RATERO : Yet another word for a thief (note. 'choro' also). This word refers more directly to petty thieves and pickpockets, the type you need to watch out for in downtown Lima.

Ex. Tengan cuidado con las carteras cuando estén en el centro de Lima, hay muchos rateros. (Be careful with handbags when you are in the centre of Lima, there are lots of pickpockets.)

RAYADO : From the verb 'rayar' which means to scratch, this past tense means scratched, which in slang is used to describe someone as either angry or mad. Can be used in place of 'enojado' or 'enfadado'.

Ex. Enrique está rayado, nadie le invitó al tono. (Enrique is angry, nobody invited him to the party.)

RESACA : This is the equivalent of a hangover. It is actually used in a number of Spanish speaking countries you will be pleased to know, and if you have too many pisco sours (the famous local drink in Perú) you will be sure to have a 'resaca' en Perú also.

Ex. Tengo resaca, me tomé cinco pisco sour anoche. (I have a hangover, I drank five pisco sours last night.)

REGALONA : This word is derived from the Spanish verb 'regalar' which is to gift. It refers specifically to the girls that gift themselves to guys. That is to say they basically throw themselves at guys. Many of these in the Miraflores neighborhood in Lima will be 'bricheras' also.

Ex. Elena es una regalona, siempre se acerca a los gringos para bailar.. (Elena es a 'regalona' she always approaches the gringos to dance.)

RICHI : Another word for food or 'comida'. It can be used interchangeable with 'jama' or 'comida'.

Ex. La richi ponja en Perú es muy deliciosa, porque el pescado allí es muy bueno. (The Japanese food in Peru is very delicious because the fish there is very good.)

ROCHE : This is used to replace 'vengüenza' in Perú, meaning shame or embarrassment.

Ex. Se me salió el zapato y mi media estaba con hueco, que tal roche. (My shoe fell off and my sock had a hole in it, how embarrassing.)

ROSQUETE : This translates as 'poof', although being slightly softer than calling somebody gay it is used in the same context.

Ex. Felipe es un rosquete, no va a venir al tono esta noche. (Felipe is a poof, he is no going to come to the party tonight.)

RUCA : This is another way to say 'puta' or prostitute. It is a little softer than saying 'puta' and is not used in place of 'puta' when saying 'puta madre' for example. It is kind of like saying 'hooker' in English.

Ex. Hay muchas rucas en la calle de las pizzas. (There are a lot of hookers in the 'calle de las pizzas' : actually this is a fact if you are ever in Miraflores in Lima you will be sure to notice.)

S

SACAR LA VUELTA : This is the act of a guy deceiving his wife or girlfriend by going with another women.

Ex. El novio de Elena le sacó la vuelta con una moza. (Elena's boyfriend deceived her with a waitress.)

SALADO : Bad luck or misfortune. This literally translates as 'salted'.

Ex. Estoy bien salado, ayer me chocó el carro y hace sólo dos semanas lo había comprado. (I am so unlucky, yesterday I crashed my car and after having only bought it two weeks ago.)

SAPO : Literally translating as a toad, this surprisingly means quite the opposite. If you call or refer to somebody as a 'sapo', you are saying that they are alert, sharp, or intelligent. Just don't use this one in Colombia, as it means something completely different (a grass, a snitch.)

Ex. Raul es muy sapo, siempre obtiene las mejores calificaciones en el colegio. (Raul is very smart, he is always getting the best grades in the college.)

SENCILLAR : This is to change money (notes) into smaller denominations, normally into coins.

Ex. ¿Me puedes sencillar un billete de 20 soles? (Can you give me change for a 20 sol note?)

SOBÓN : This is the same 'chupa medias' meaning ass kisser, but it is used more frequently than 'chupa medias' in Perú.

Ex. Elena es una sobón, todos los días lleva una manzana para la profesora. (Elena is a kiss ass, everyday she brings the teacher an apple.)

SOPA (SOPERO) : Literally 'sopa' translates as soup in English. But, in slang it is used to describe cunnilingus, and a man who gives it is called a 'sopero'.

Ex. Mi novia le gusta mucho a tener sopa. (My girlfriend likes a lot to have cunnilingus.)

SOPLÓN : This means a grass or a snitch, it is derived for the verb 'soplar' which is to blow or to whisper.

Ex. Felipe es un soplón, siempre dijera al profesor si no habríamos hecho la tarea. (Felipe is a snitch, he will always tell the teacher if we have not done the homework.)

SUZUKI : This is used as a play on the Spanish word for dirty (sucio) and is used exactly that context, to call something or someone dirty (unclean).

Ex.Tu caña está suzuki. (Your car is dirty.)

T

TABA : Meaning shoe, this refers to somebody as clumsy, slow and without and skills. 'Taba' replaces 'torpe' in slang.

Ex. Alejendra es taba, siempre deja caer los platos al suelo. (Alejendra is clumsy, she is always dropping the plates on the floor.)

TARRO : This is used to call a women's ass. The word translates literally as jar or pot.

Ex. Qué buen tarro tiene la hermana de Pablo. (What a great ass Pablo's sister has.)

TELO : This is also used in a few other Spanish speaking countries, particularly in Argentina. It is a play on the letter order and comes from hotel, which is what it actually means. It is used more often to describe the short term or short stay hotels where you can rent a room for a few hours. These are common in Peru as the majority of people live with their parents until they get married, which means that many live a home until they are 30 years old. You don't want to bring your one-night stands back to your parents house, so you go to a 'telo'.

Ex. Te sugiero cuando vayas a tener un choque y fuga que vayas a un telo, sería más discreto. (I suggest when you are going to have a one night stand you go to a 'telo' it would be more discreet.)

TERRUCO : Peru has had it's fair share of problems internally with terrorists, so it is hardly surprising that there is a slang word for 'terrorist'.

Ex. Hace unos años habían problemas con los terrucos en el campo. (Some years ago there were problems with terrorists in the countryside.)

TIGRE : Literally a 'tiger', this is used to describe somebody who is the best, or who has the best skill in something.

Ex. Soy un tigre en la cancha de football. (I am the best on the football field.)

TOCAR LA CORNETA : Fellatio, or as it translates literally 'to play the cornet'. What a poetic way of saying 'giving head'.

Ex. Me gusta cuando mi novia toque la corneta. (I like it when my girlfriend gives head.)

TOMBO : This is the equivalent of saying cop in English. It is the slang for a police office.

Ex. Todos los tombos les gustan las coimas. (All the cops like bribes.)

TONEAR : A verb in slang meaning to party.

Ex. Vamos a tonear esta noche en Lima (Lets go party tonight in Lima.)

TONO : Literally meaning tone, this is used in place of 'fiesta' or party. And to say that it is a big party you will sometimes here the word morph into 'tonazo'.

Ex. Anoche el tono era muy divertido, me gustó mucho. (Last night the party was a lot of fun, I enjoyed it.)

TROCA : This is one way of saying whorehouse or knocking shop.

Ex. Vamos al troca, quiero cachar. (Lets go to the whorehouse, I want to have sex.)

V

VACILAR : Literally this means 'to hesitate', however in Perú it is used in place of 'gustar' (to like).

Ex. Me vacila tu vestido, es bacán. (I like your dress, it's cool.)

VIEJO (A) : Literally meaning old it's equivalent in English is the old folks, meaning the parents.

Ex. Mi viejo estaba enojado conmigo porque llegué tarde para la fiesta de su cumpleaños. (My father was angry with me because I arrived late for his birthday party.)

Y

YARA : This is a word of warning, it is the same as saying 'watch out', or be careful.

Ex. ¡Yara! Tenga cuidado cuando cruce la calle, hay muchos carros. (Hey watch out! Be careful when you cross the street there are a lot of cars.)

YUCA : The literal translation is fairly obvious, yucca, the plant. However, in the singular form it is also used to describe difficult or something that has a very low probability of success.

Ex. Está yuca sacarse el premio son muchos particpantes. (There is almost no chance of wining this prize, there are lots of participants.)

YUCAS : The literal translation would be the plural of 'yuca'. But, this has nothing to do with 'yuca', it refers to legs (piernas) of all things.

Ex. Qué buenas yucas tiene Paola. (What great legs Paola has.)

YUNTA : This is another word used to call a friend in Perú. Can be interchanged with 'pata', 'amigo' and 'causa' for example.

Ex. Jose es mi yunta. (Jose is my friend.)

Z

ZANAHORIA : Literally this means carrot, however it is used to describe somebody that has no vices, for example somebody that does not drink, does not smoke, does not stay up late watching TV. It kind of translates to somebody who is a square in English.

Ex. Carla es una zanahoria, ni fuma, ni chupa y siempre se va temprano. (Carla is a Zanahoria, she does not smoke, does not drink, and always leaves early.)

Other books by this author

A Taste of Peru. The Best Peruvian Recipes.

A Taste of Peru, here you have to the chance to try some of the best and most popular Peruvian recipes at home. There are many great recipes to choose from.

This book covers starters, soups, sauces (salsas), main dishes, desserts and drinks to give you a truly Peruvian experience.

1001 Spanish Flash Cards : Spanish Vocabulary Builder

Spanish Flash cards are a great way to quickly and painlessly improve your Spanish vocabulary. Use this cards to memorise new Spanish words efficiently.

Both of these books are available at amazon.com.

Made in the USA
San Bernardino, CA
09 December 2019